"*I can't wait to eat!*" Burhaan said. "Our trip was way too long."

"It was only about three hours," his father reminded him.

"Well, that was long enough for me," replied Burhaan.

"The food will be ready in a little while," his aunt called out from the kitchen.

His cousins, who were gathering by the door, yelled out, "Hey, Burhaan! We can all play around in the backyard until the food is ready. Let's go!"

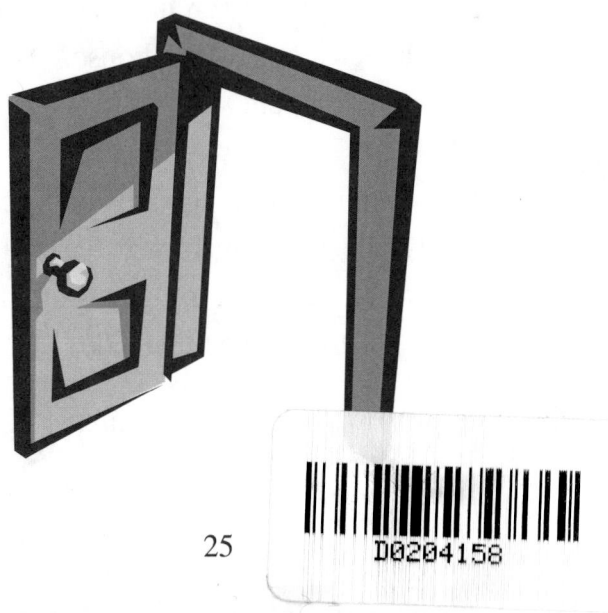

"That's a good idea," said his uncle.

"Remember, don't be late because we're all going out after lunch, and please don't get too dirty," remarked Burhaan's aunt.

"Uh-huh," was the response that she received from her children. Burhaan replied, "*Insha'llah*, we'll be back on time. *Assalamu alaikum!*"

His father responded clearly, "*Wa alaikum assalam.*" But the rest of the family didn't reply with any Islamic greeting at all. Burhaan shrugged it off. Maybe they didn't hear so well.

When Burhaan turned around to leave, he found his cousins were already out of the house. He had to run quickly to catch up to them.

All of the children ran towards a fence with a hole in it. Each one made their way through the opening quickly. When the sixth child was through, they all looked at Burhaan who was still on the other side.

"What are you waiting for?" said Kareem, the oldest child.

"I thought you told your parents that we were going to play in the backyard."

"I told them we were going to play *around* the backyard. Anyway, since this fence doesn't completely close off the backyard, this side could be considered our backyard, too."

"But that's lying," said Burhaan. "They think that we're going to stay closer to the house."

Kareem's younger brothers and sister were shocked that Burhaan was even questioning their older brother.

Taken aback himself, Kareem responded by saying, "Listen, as long as we get back on time, we'll be fine. Look, if you're too scared to come with us, then just stay there all by yourself!"

Burhaan though about it. His cousin's argument did sound fairly okay. If they arrived back in time, would it be that bad?

"Are you coming or not?" asked Kareem.

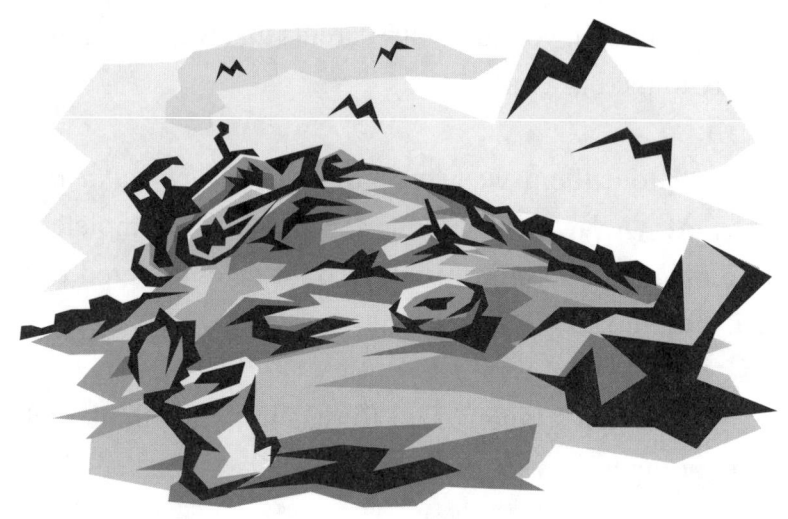

"Yeah, I'm coming." Burhaan slipped through the hole and followed his six cousins as they made their way through a dumping ground filled with muddy hills and mounds of garbage, each picking up rocks along the way.

All the children just ran around everywhere, not worrying about getting dirty. Burhaan, on the other hand, walked very carefully so that he wouldn't get dirty.

Finally, they cleared through the field and came out on a street with a row of houses on the other side. Kareem asked Burhaan, "Hey, where are all your rocks?"

"What do you mean?"

"Well, how are you going to break things without having any rocks? Didn't you see us picking up all those rocks back there?"

Burhaan was stunned. He looked at each child, their faces and clothes all dirty, holding rocks in both hands. Even the youngest sister, Reshma, held a small rock. "I don't want to do that. I thought we were going to play-fight. You know, pretend to fight in some famous battles or something." Burhaan hoped that Kareem's response would be a good one. It wasn't.

Kareem looked at Burhaan angrily. It was the second time that Burhaan had questioned him. Holding one of the rocks at Burhaan's head, he screamed, "Why do you want to pretend to do damage when you can do it for real?! Now pick up a rock and get ready to throw it, or I'll hit you! Do you hear me!"

Burhaan held back his fear. He had never been threatened before. He didn't know what scared him more, the rock that was just inches away from his head or the person holding it. Then, Burhaan realized who he feared even more than Kareem, Allah. Burhaan would not be a part of anything he knew Allah wouldn't like.

"By Allah, I will not do what you tell me to," Burhaan finally said calmly.

"Forget Allah! Just do as I say!"

Burhaan's eyes became wide, and he slowly uttered, "*Astagh-fir-rullah!*" "*Allah forgive!*"

The second oldest, Khalil, interrupted, "Look, just forget about him. We're wasting time. Just leave him here. He's not going anywhere. He doesn't even know the way home."

Burhaan stood up tall and said, "*You who believe! Be afraid of Allah and be with those who are true.*" With that said, Burhaan turned around and started walking away from them.

"*Are you crazy!* You don't even know the way home!"

With a crooked smile Kareem said, "Let him go. He's the one who's lost, not us." They all faced the row of homes and began to throw their rocks at the windows.

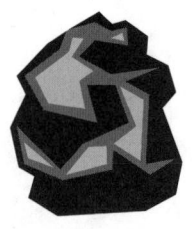

Burhaan wasn't too worried about making it home. Instead of picking up rocks like his cousins, he had been memorizing landmarks. After a while he finally made it back to the fence with the hole in it. With the smell of food in the air, Burhaan was on time for lunch, too.

But what would he tell his father, uncle, and aunt when he entered the house alone? Before he could answer that question, he heard a lot of yelling coming from the other side of the house.

"I want you to beat them good!" yelled one old man.

"We finally caught them! Throw them *and their parents* in jail!" yelled an old woman. Many voices called out in agreement.

Burhaan walked carefully to the wall of the house and looked around the corner to where the front door was. There he saw a crowd of people with angry faces and closed fists. In front of them stood all six cousins, lined up against the wall of the house with their heads bent downward in shame. A police officer was watching them, so they wouldn't move. Some were crying loudly. Kareem just stood there looking at the people who were shouting.

His aunt and uncle were there talking with several other police officers who were showing them all the complaint reports they had received.

Burhaan's aunt and uncle both looked ashamed and scared.

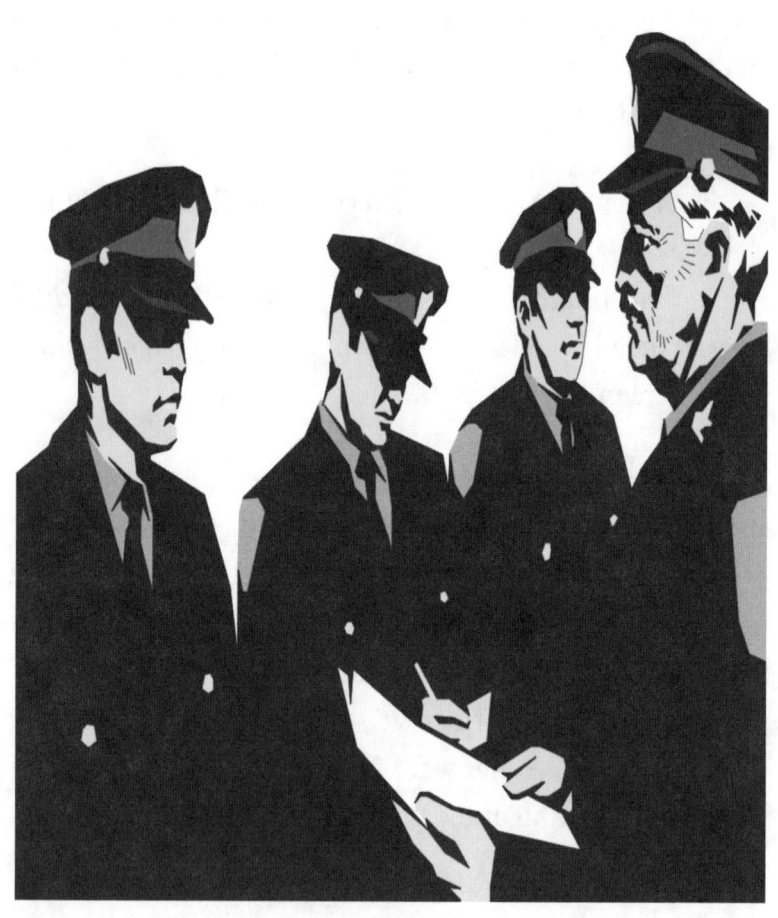

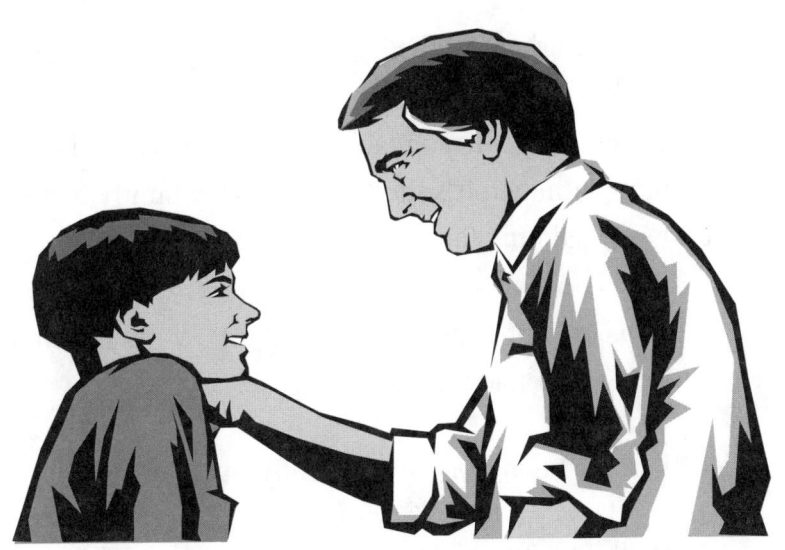

Burhaan's father saw Burhaan peeking around the corner and quickly walked over to him and picked him up and hugged him. *"Assalamu 'alaikum,* my child! Where were you? What happened? Are you all right? Were you with them when they broke those people's windows?"

Burhaan explained the whole thing to his father, and to a police officer who came to talk to him. Every once in a while they'd look at the young children and then at the parents.

After an hour, Burhaan and his father were on their way back home. They were both quiet for a while. Then his father spoke, "I guess you had an interesting day?"

"Yes," Burhaan sighed.

"I knew there was something wrong when they didn't want to pray with me. It's sad to see a whole family forget about Islam," said his father.

Burhaan continued, "After seeing how my cousins acted, I knew they had no Iman."

"I'm glad that you didn't do anything wrong."

"Well, you and Ummi are doing a good job."

His father thought for a second and said, "Alhumdulillah."

"Oh, Abu?"

"Yes, Burhaan. What is it?"

"I'm still hungry."

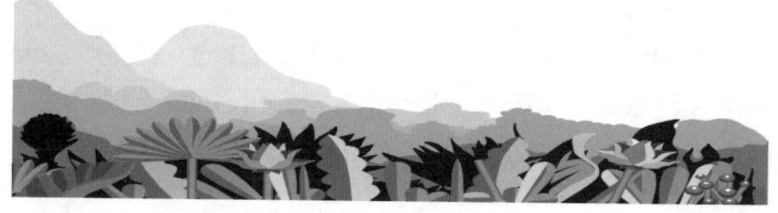

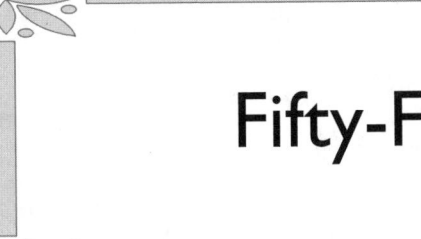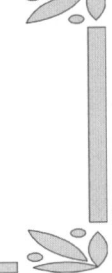

Fifty-Fifty

"Who is the one that sings nasheeds?"

Burhaan . . Burhaan

"Who is the one that does good deeds?"

Burhaan . . Burhaan

"Who is the one that loves tawheed,"

"and prays to Allah when in need?"

"Who is the one that sings nasheeds?"

Burhaan . . Burhaan

"Remember class, we're going to have a test next week. You all have plenty of time to study for it, so I'm sure you'll all do well, insha'llah." Burhaan's teacher looked upon her class and saw her words bounce off the children's heads and onto the floor. *"Did you all hear me?"* she asked.

All of the children responded in a dry voice, "Yes, sister Nadia."

"Burhaan. Burhaan. Burhaan Khan!" repeated the teacher. Burhaan, however, was very busy staring out the window, daydreaming. *"...and if we moved our horses to the left, we would stop the enemy from..."* he said from under his breath.

The teacher moved closer to Burhaan until she was standing right in front of him.

"So, Burhaan. What are you supposed to be ready for next week?"

"Huh? What?"

"Burhaan?"

"Yes, sister Nadia?"

"What do you have to say about yourself?" she demanded.

"Huh?"

Sister Nadia stared at him and asked, "Will you be ready for it?"

"For what?"

"The test."

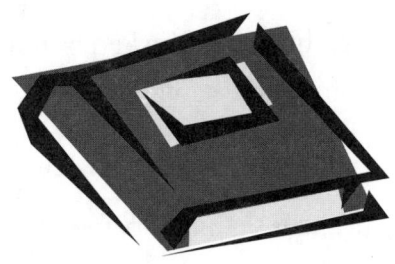

"What test?"

"The test that you will be taking next Friday."

"We have a test on Friday?"

"Yes, Burhaan Khan, you have a test next week on Friday. I highly suggest you study very hard for it. The test will be difficult." The teacher turned around, made a du'a with the class, and dismissed them for the day.

Burhaan didn't take what the teacher said too seriously. He was already a pretty good student. How difficult could this next test be? He just swung his books and skipped over rocks and hills while he went home.

Days passed, and Burhaan did not study for his exam. While he did do his homework, he did not go over the things that would be on the test. He just played a lot.

Even though his parents asked him if he needed any help with his school work, he would always respond, "It's okay. I have it all under control."

The day of the test finally came. Before the papers were given out, Burhaan made a quick du'a for Allah to help him pass the test. With that done, he turned over his question sheet and started.

Burhaan was the first student to finish. The teacher had asked him to check his test over again. Burhaan responded, "I don't need to. This was a very easy test."

"I'm happy that you think you did so well."

"Sister. Since I finished so early, can you please check my test now?"

Although the teacher didn't like to tell students what their grade was before all the tests were checked, she made an exception for Burhaan.

From his seat, Burhaan watched the teacher take out her red pen and start to read his exam. He could see her wrist make sharp movements upward then down at each line as she went down the list of questions.

One "**X**" mark after the other, he felt sweat build up around his brow. It all ended with one quick sweep of her hand in a circular shaped motion at the top of his page. She shook her head slowly, raised it, then said, "Burhaan, please come here to get your test."

Burhaan quietly got out of his seat. There were still some students taking the test. He was hoping no one saw the marks that the teacher was making on his test. As he passed each row, the other students' heads went up, one after the other. They had all seen the teacher's face as she graded the test. Burhaan took slow steps towards her desk, hoping that it would change things. It didn't.

She folded the exam and gave it back to him.

He didn't bother opening up the paper to see his grade. He could see the big, red zero from the back of the paper. As he walked back to his desk, he hoped that the grade would change. It didn't. Burhaan slowly sat down while the rest of the class began to hand in their exams.

When class ended and the other students had left the room, sister Nadia asked Burhaan to come to her desk.

Burhaan knew the question she was going to ask before she started to speak.

"Burhaan, did you study for the exam?"

He fidgeted a bit. He didn't want to tell her that he hadn't studied, but he also didn't want to lie to her. "No, I didn't study."

"Did you have enough time to study?"

"Yes, I had plenty of time."

She continued to look at him. He stood there, awkwardly. She then asked the question that all teachers ask of all students. "Then, why didn't you study?"

Burhaan thought for a minute and gave her an honest answer. "The work seemed very easy to me.

I was doing well on all of the tests before this. I thought that if I made a du'a to Allah, He would just help me out. I mean, He can do anything, right?"

Sister Nadia smiled at his answer. "Burhaan, while Allah can do anything, you must understand that we cannot take His help for granted. We can't just sit back and expect Allah to do everything for us. He gave us life, but we're in charge of it. Achievements aren't given to us for free. It's as if you put effort into baking a cake, but I'm the one who gets all the credit for it. It wouldn't be fair. You should be rewarded for your efforts."

"But isn't making a Du'a or praying to Allah enough of an effort?"

"Not really because our actions show how honest we are about our intentions for an act. We are the one's who make the choice on the way we work with what Allah gave us. When you study for an exam, you are showing Allah that you mean and believe in the du'a you recited."

"And what if I fail?"

"If you fail, it's not the end of the world. Allah did not fail you. Remember, Allah has given you a mind, a body, a way to express yourself. You have the ability to grow in many ways. Allah has already given you a beautiful life to work with. The rest is up to you. Remember what the Qur'an says, 'Allah rewards those who make an effort.'"

Burhaan had heard that ayah before. It never made more sense to him than it did now.

He asked her if he could take the test over again. She told him "yes," but it would be a different test. Burhaan thanked her, said his salam, and went home.

For the next two days, all Burhaan did was study, with some time to rest in between. The next day, he ate his lunch in the class and took the test while other students played.

Before the students returned to the class room, sister Nadia checked the exam. This time there were fewer criss-crossed hand movements. When Burhaan received his test, he smiled. Burhaan had passed with a very good grade.

"Did it take a lot of work for you to study, Burhaan?"

Still staring at his test Burhaan responded, "Not really. All I did was take my time and study the best I could."

As the teacher was writing the next lesson on the board she said, "Do you think you can keep up that kind of attitude through the rest of your school years?"

Burhaan looked at his grade again then at the teacher and said, "Insha'llah."

A Special Eid

"Who's the one that loves to read?"

Burhaan . . Burhaan

"Who tries his best to live his creed?"

Burhaan . . Burhaan

"Who is the one that helps us shout?"

"Who is the one who never pouts?"

"Who is the one that learns tawheed?"

Burhaan . . Burhaan

"id Mubarak!... Eid Mubarak!" The phrase echoed through out the Masjid all morning. The Salat was finished, and people were making plans with each other for that afternoon's festivities.

Burhaan was with his friend, Fadil. Both of their families were going to get together later in the day at Fadil's house. Because Fadil lived only a few streets away from the Masjid, Burhaan and Fadil asked their parents if they could walk home. They would be sure to arrive before lunch started.

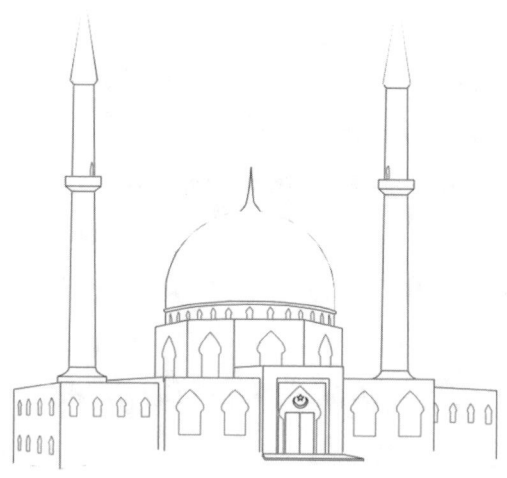

Then, with their parent's permission, they both left.

As they passed by house after house down the street, they spoke about the things they did to keep their mind off food during the fast. Each of their stories became more creative as they spoke.

"Well, I counted all of the tiles on the roof and all of the bricks on our house," declared Fadil.

Not be out done, Burhaan added a method of his own. "Oh, yeah? I've been counting my footsteps since the fast began!"

Fadil looked at him in shock.

"What number are you up to now?"

Burhaan shook his head a little and waved his hand in the air. "Well, you of course know that the fast is over.

"So, I technically stopped when we finished the Salat. I did, however, reach footstep number 643,892!"

"Wow," said Fadil, "that's incredible."

Burhaan cracked a broad smile and said, "Why, thank you very much. It was really nothing."

"How did you manage counting when you had to run or something?" asked Fadil with eyes wide open.

"That was a little difficult, but I can teach you."

"Gee, thanks."

"No problem. We'll squeeze it in during our Arabic lessons."

As they walked near a small patch of bushes they noticed a tree ahead of them that had something strange on it. When they moved closer to look they saw a cat clinging to the side of the tree about five feet up. It seemed frozen, as if it were going to leap at any moment. They stopped just behind some bushes to watch the animal.

"That looks so cool," said Fadil.

"Yeah," agreed Burhaan, "look how still it is."

"What is it looking at?" asked Fadil.

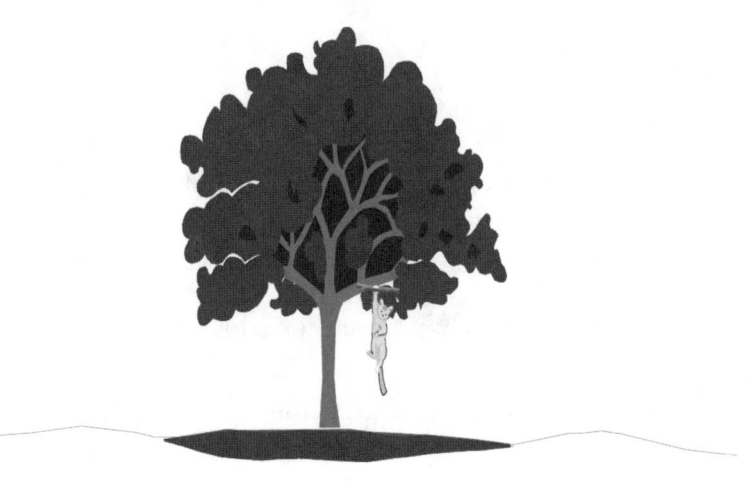

Burhaan looked around and replied, "I'm not sure. Then again, cats have pretty good eye sight. We probably couldn't even see what it was looking at if we wanted to."

A long time had passed, and the cat hadn't moved at all. Burhaan and Fadil were getting tired.

"When is it going to jump?" Fadil asked.

"I'm not sure, but we should check on it."

Burhaan made his way over to the tree slowly so as not to disturb the cat.

Peeking over the bush, Fadil yelled out, "Is it okay?"

"I'm not sure. Let me check."

Burhaan picked up a small pebble and tossed it lightly at the tree. The cat's tale moved.

"He's alive! He's alive!" cried Burhaan.

"Why isn't he jumping off?" shouted Fadil.

"Hold on. I'm going to get closer."

Because the tree was in somebody's yard, Burhaan was nervous about trespassing.

Burhaan yelled towards the house to try and catch the attention of the owners inside. "Hey! Hey!"

No one came to any window or door. Burhaan looked again at the cat and saw it shift slightly.

"I think it's caught on something!" he called back to Fadil.

"What should we do?"

Burhaan thought. He knew that he needed permission before he went on someone else's property, but he couldn't leave the cat there not knowing if it could ever get away.

"Come on Fadil. We've got to help," cried Burhaan.

Fadil came from behind the bushes and climbed with Burhaan over the fence. They both continued to call the owner to let him or her know that they were there. No answer again. They must not be home.

When they got closer to the cat, they saw that it was caught in many fish hooks that were hanging down from the tree on metal wire. At the first sight of the cat Fadil almost got sick. Burhaan just stared at the poor animal as it hung there, trying to pull itself free. There were hooks through its paws, face and legs. It turned its face to see the two boys looking at it and looked startled.

"What are we going to do, Burhaan?" asked Fadil, not wanting to look at the horrible sight.

"We have to save it."

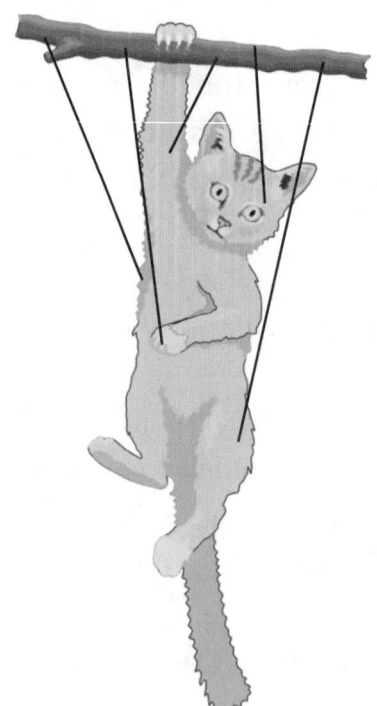

The cat hung there nervously. Every time it moved, the hooks would pull at its flesh.

They both could tell it was exhausted.

"He must have been hanging here for hours," said Fadil.

"Ya-Allah," whispered Burhaan.

They both thought about what they could do to help the cat.

"What if we try to take him off the tree slowly?" asked Fadil.

"We can't do that," responded Burhaan. "There are so many hooks inside his body that if we try to pull him off, even very slowly, they'll hurt him even more!"

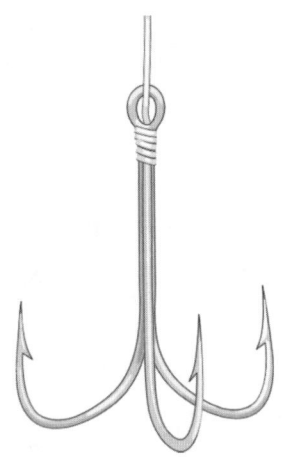

"Why would anyone put fish hooks on a tree?" asked Fadil.

They both looked around and noticed that those "traps" were on every tree in the yard. They also saw that all the trees were fruit trees.

With a slow shake of his head, Burhaan finally said, "I guess this person doesn't want anyone or anything to take any fruit off the trees."

"But this seems so *horrible!*" shouted Fadil as he looked up at the helpless cat, hanging painfully with hooks through its body.

"I know."

After looking at the wires, and how they were attached to the tree, Fadil finally yelled out, "I got it. I got it. If one of us holds the cat, the other one can cut the wires down!"

"How are we going to cut them?"

"Well, don't you have your pocket knife with you?"

"Let me check."

Burhaan reached into every pocket and felt for his pocket knife. When his fingers folded around it he pulled it out quickly.

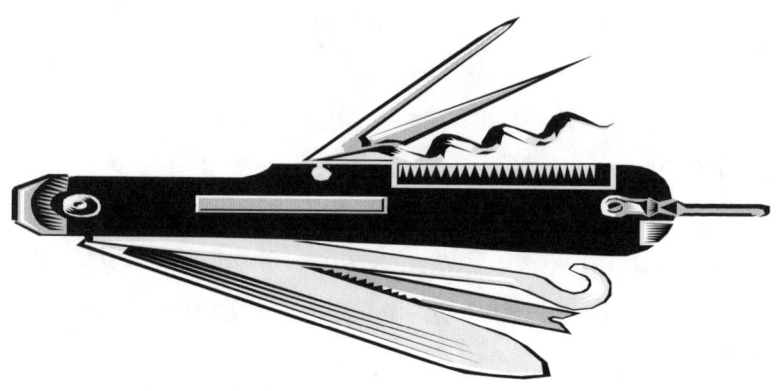

Burhaan then asked, "Who's going to hold on to the cat, and who's going to do the cutting?"

Fadil answered, "I'll hold on to him."

Burhaan was surprised and said, "But you might get sick. Are you sure?"

Fadil told Burhaan that the cat was in more pain than he himself was in. He will tough it out for the sake of the cat.

"Besides, Burhaan, you're the only one who can reach the wires to cut them."

They both got ready. Burhaan distracted the animal while Fadil got behind it to hold it. When the cat turned its head towards Burhaan, Fadil quickly grabbed its back and neck.

Since the cat was slightly high on the tree, Fadil had to reach up on his tip-toes to hold him firmly. The cat turned his head and for a moment stared at the human holding onto him. Burhaan began climbing the tree.

Because the hooks spread out a lot, it was hard for Burhaan to grab at the wires that held up the hooks. He would have to reach a branch and try to climb up the tree that way.

"Are you okay?" asked Fadil.

"Yea, but this is going to be harder than we thought."

Burhaan tried to reach for a strong branch because if he didn't, he might fall into the hooks himself. He finally managed to grab onto a low, strong branch. He slowly pulled himself up, trying not to shake the tree too much. Fadil, meanwhile, tried to keep the cat calm.

He could feel its heart beating quickly in the palms of his hands. He also felt the strain in his own back and legs.

"I can't imagine being in this position for a long time," Fadil said.

"Yeah. Imagine how the cat feels," Burhaan said.

Burhaan made it to a good branch. Then, after looking at the wires, he then realized that there was a problem.

"Hey, Fadil? If I cut these wires, the cat is going to fall on you. We have to be careful about this."

"Should I jump out of the way before you finish cutting the last wire?"

Burhaan thought for a while and said, "I don't think that would work because if you did that, the cat would probably land on the ground and run away with its body still full of hooks."

"Can't we just cut the hooks instead?"

Burhaan looked at the hooks. "No, they're too thick. I'll have to cut the wires one by one. As I cut each one, the cat will come slowly lower. Bring it down with you and then put it on the ground and hold it," Burhaan said.

Fadil's arms and feet were getting very tired. "How many wires are there, Burhaan?"

After counting, Burhaan said, "Nine."

Burhaan looked at Fadil and told him to hold on to the cat as hard and as firm as he could.

"Remember, the cat has been up here longer than either one of us and may panic and scratch you."

When Fadil thought about that and felt the cat's heart beating, he tightened his back, legs and arms as if he were the cat's pillar. After that, Fadil no longer felt pain.

Burhaan wanted to make sure that the first hook he cut was the right one. If he cut a wrong one, the animal's weight could shift too quickly, and the cat could become even more hurt.

"How does he feel to you ? I mean, which wire should I cut first?"

Fadil suggested that Burhaan cut the three that were hooked to the cat's head.

"Then, I'll work on the legs."

"Yeah, that way he won't be hanging in this weird position."

Burhaan made the first cut. The cat started to move around wildly, trying to escape.

"Don't worry, Fadil," Burhaan said. "He's just scared. He'll calm down after a little while."

Burhaan was right. The cat began to calm down. Even the heart beat started to slow down. Fadil started to rub the cat's neck with his thumb to comfort him.

When the hooks in the paws were cut, the cat's legs fell limply.

Fadil said, "I think he wants to sleep. He looks really tired."

"Don't worry. I'm almost finished."

Burhaan cut the last wire, and Fadil lowered the cat to the ground very slowly and held his body carefully.

Burhaan made his way back to the strong branch and climbed down. When he got to both of them, Fadil was crying. Burhaan moved around to where the cat lay. The hooks still covered its small, bloody body.

Fadil looked up at Burhaan and whispered through tears, "I felt his heart stop. He stopped breathing. I...I..."

Burhaan stood there silently and then began to cry as well.

"We both tried, Fadil. We both did our best to save him."

"I know, but it hurts. Why did he have to die?"

Burhaan walked over to Fadil and put his arm around his shoulder. "Fadil, we stopped his pain. We ended its suffering. Think about how many people walked by today and just left him there. We did a good deed. We ended pain and suffering in one of Allah's creatures."

"I know. But it just hurts. It hurts a lot."

"Yeah, I know. It hurts me, too," replied Burhaan.

They both sat there for a while. It was getting late, and they both had to go home. Burhaan and Fadil quietly began to dig a hole for the body under the shade of the fruit tree where they found him.

"When we get home," said Burhaan, "we'll tell our parents about this place. We can't let any other animals die this way just because some person wants to protect his fruit trees."

"Okay," whispered Fadil.

When they finished covering up the body with soil, both walked towards the fence. But before they left, Burhaan placed his finger into the soil and used it to trace out a name for this unmarked grave. In tiny letters he wrote the name, *Eid*.

THE END

Selected Titles Available From IBTS

Ahmad Deen and the Jinn at Shaolin
By Yahiya Emerick

A once in a lifetime chance! Ahmad Deen is one of ten lucky students in his school who gets an all-expense paid trip to China. But instead of getting a history lesson, Ahmad may become a victim *of history* as he is thrust in the middle of a bizarre web of superstition, corruption and ancient hatreds that seek to destroy all who interfere.

Who kidnapped his room-mate? What clue can only be found in the Shaolin Temple? How will Ahmad learn the Kung-Fu skills he'll need to defeat the powers of darkness. or will he fall prey to the mysterious *Jinn at Shaolin?* Illustrated, 120 pages.

The Army of Lions
By Qasim Najar

Get ready for swashbuckling and deeds of valor at its finest! The Army of Lions is coming! Take yourself back to the days when a believer and his faith could destroy every evil tyrant, when the brave and true could sweep over the plains and cities of the world and make them take notice. If you're impressed by unswerving determination and faith that conquers all, then be prepared to join the Army of Lions! A full length fiction novel set in the golden age of Islam. Illustrated, 176 pages.

Layla Deen and the Case of the Ramadan Rogue
By Yahiya Emerick

Somebody's trying to ruin her Ramadan! Layla Deen and her family were just settling in to break a long days fast when their mother came running from the kitchen and cried, *"Someone stole the food for Iftar!"* Layla knew it was a terrible crime and decided to get to the bottom of this mystery. See what happens! Illustrated. 54 pages.

Isabella: A Girl of Muslim Spain

By Yahiya Emerick

A classic tale about a young girl who finds Islam, and danger, amidst the harrowing religious conflicts of medieval Muslim Spain.

Experience firsthand what life was like in the splendid Muslim city of Cordoba. See through the eyes of Isabella as she struggles with her father's Christian beliefs and finds that life is not always as easy as people think. Embark on a journey into history, into the heart, as you follow her path from darkness into light.

Highly recommended for teenagers and young adults. A sensitive and realistic portrayal from a unique point of view unlike anything you have ever read. Illustrated, 130 pages.

Ahmad Deen and the Curse of the Aztec Warrior

By Yahiya Emerick

Where is he? Ahmad Deen and his sister Layla thought they were getting a nice vacation in tropical Mexico. But what they're really going to get is a hair-raising race against time to save their father from becoming the next victim of an ancient, bloody ritual!

How can Ahmad save his father *and* deal with his bratty sister at the same time? To make matters worse, no one seems to want to help them find the mysterious lost city that may hold the key to their father's whereabouts. And then there's that jungle guide with the strangely familiar jacket. Are they brave enough—or crazy enough, to take on the *Curse of the Aztec Warrior?* Illustrated, 54 pages.

Learning About Islam

By Yahiya Emerick

A real textbook of Islamic Studies for use in grades 3-5. This textbook covers all the fundamentals of Islam and is arranged into clearly defined lessons and units. A stunningly beautiful book by the same author as the popular textbook for older children, "What Islam is All About." Illustrated, BW, 224 pages.